5B

Reach
HIGHER

Practice Book

NATIONAL
GEOGRAPHIC
LEARNING

Australia · Brazil · Mexico · Singapore · United Kingdom · United States

National Geographic Learning,
a Cengage Company

Reach Higher Practice Book 5B

Publisher, Content-based English: Erik Gundersen

Associate Director, R&D: Barnaby Pelter

Senior Development Editors:
   Jacqueline Eu
   Ranjini Fonseka
   Kelsey Zhang

Development Editor: Rayne Ngoi

Director of Global Marketing: Ian Martin

Heads of Regional Marketing:
   Charlotte Ellis (Europe, Middle East and Africa)
   Kiel Hamm (Asia)
   Irina Pereyra (Latin America)

Product Marketing Manager: David Spain

Senior Production Controller: Tan Jin Hock

Senior Media Researcher (Covers): Leila Hishmeh

Senior Designer: Lisa Trager

Director, Operations: Jason Seigel

Operations Support:
   Rebecca Barbush
   Drew Robertson
   Caroline Stephenson
   Nicholas Yeaton

Manufacturing Planner: Mary Beth Hennebury

Publishing Consultancy and Composition:
   MPS North America LLC

For permission to use material from this text or product,
submit all requests online at **cengage.com/permissions**
Further permissions questions can be emailed to
permissionrequest@cengage.com

ISBN-13: 978-0-357-36702-5

National Geographic Learning
200 Pier Four Blvd
Boston, MA 02210
USA

Locate your local office at **international.cengage.com/region**

Visit National Geographic Learning online at **ELTNGL.com**
Visit our corporate website at **www.cengage.com**

Printed in the United States of America
Print Number: 07   Print Year: 2022

Contents

Unit 7: Talking About Trash

Unit 8: One Idea

Unit Concept Map

Every Drop

Make a concept map with the answers to the Big Question: Why is water so important?

Why is water so important?

Thinking Map

Problems from Drought

Think about how droughts affect Elena's family and farm. Then write
the main ideas and details.

I. _____

   A. _____

   B. _____

II. _____

   A. _____

   B. _____

III. _____

   A. _____

   B. _____

Talk with a partner about ways water is important to Elena's
family.

Grammar

Water Worries

Grammar Rules Adjectives

1. Add **-er** to an adjective to compare two things.
2. Add **-est** to an adjective to compare three or more things.

Complete each sentence. Add -er or -est to the word below the line.

1. Our farm is the _____ one in our area.
   old

2. Our well is by far the _____ .
   deep

3. This year, the water level was _____ than it should be.
   low

4. We were worried our crops would be _____ than they were
   small

   last year.

5. Luckily, our corn grew _____ than we thought it would.
   tall

   With a partner, change each sentence with an **-er** word to a
   sentence with an **-est** word.

"One Well"

Listen as your teacher reads. Follow with your finger.

1

Most of the Earth's surface is covered with water. Surface water is found in oceans, lakes, rivers, and streams.

There is also groundwater. It fills the spaces between rocks, sand, and soil.

2

Water goes through the water cycle. It evaporates into the air. As the water vapor rises, it forms tiny droplets and then becomes clouds. When the droplets get too heavy, they fall as rain or snow.

3

Plants depend on water for transpiration and photosynthesis. Animals depend on water to aid digestion, remove waste, and control temperature.

4

Not all water is accessible. Most of the water on Earth is saltwater. The distribution of fresh water across the world is not equal. Many people do not have enough fresh water. Taking action to conserve the water supply will help protect it for everyone.

Grammar

The Adjective Game

Grammar Rules Adjectives

1. To compare two things, use **more . . . than** or **less . . . than** if an adjective has three or more syllables.

2. When you compare three or more things, use **most** or **least** if the adjective has three or more syllables.

3. Some adjectives have special forms for comparing things. For example: **good**, **better**, **best**.

1. **Play with a partner.**

2. **Spin the spinner.**

3. **Read the adjective. Use it to compare either two things or three or more things.**

Make a Spinner

1. Place one loop of a paper clip over the center of the circle.

2. Push a sharp pencil through the loop and the paper.

3. Spin the paper clip around the pencil.

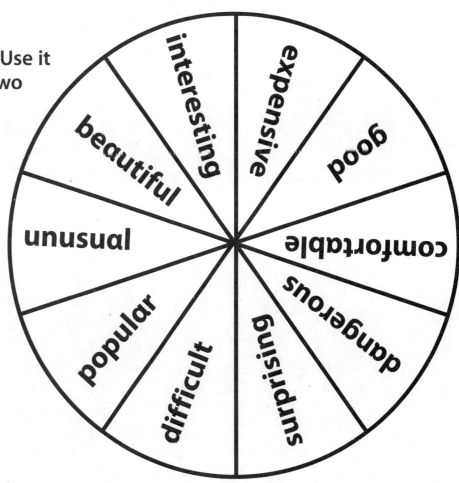

Name _____   Date _____

Vocabulary Bingo

Play Bingo using the Key Words from this unit.

Reread and Retell

"One Well"

Reread "One Well." Then write the main ideas and details.

   I. **All water on Earth is connected.**

   A. **About 70% of Earth's surface is water.**

   B. **Some water is buried deep under the ground.**

   II. **Water keeps moving through the water cycle.**

   A. **It rises from water sources as gas or vapor.**

   B. _____

   III. _____

   A. _____

   B. _____

   IV. _____

   A. _____

   B. _____

   V. _____

   A. _____

   B. _____

   VI. _____

   A. _____

   B. _____

Reread and Retell

"One Well" (continued)

VII. **Distribution of water is different around the world.**

    A. _____

    B. _____

VIII. **We use water for many things.**

    A. _____

    B. _____

    C. _____

IX. _____

    A. _____

    B. _____

X. _____

    A. _____

    B. _____

    C. _____

XI. _____

    A. _____

    B. _____

▶ **Use your outline to summarize the selection to a partner.**

Name _____ Date _____

"One Well"

Use this passage to practice reading with proper phrasing.

Imagine for a moment that all the water on Earth came from just one well.   15

This isn't as strange as it sounds. All water on Earth is connected, so there really   31

is just one source, one global well, from which we can draw all our water. Every ocean   48

wave, every lake, stream, and underground river, every raindrop and snowflake and   60

every bit of ice in glaciers and polar icecaps is a part of this global well.   76

Because it is all connected, how we treat the water in the well will affect every   92

species on the planet, now and for years to come.   102

From "One Well," page 12

Phrasing

[B] ☐ Rarely pauses while reading the text.   [A] ☐ Frequently pauses at appropriate points in the text.

[I] ☐ Occasionally pauses while reading the text.   [AH] ☐ Consistently pauses at all appropriate points in the text.

Accuracy and Rate Formula

Use the formula to measure a reader's accuracy and rate while reading aloud.

_____	−	_____	=	_____
words attempted in one minute		number of errors		words correct per minute (wcpm)

Reading Options

"Picturing the Pantanal"

Complete the double-entry log as you read "Picturing the Pantanal."

Page	What I read	What it reminds me of

Tell a partner which detail was the most interesting and why.

Compare Texts

Use the chart to compare texts.

	"Picturing the Pantanal"	"One Well"
Genre		
Topic		
Main idea	Through photos, Dr. Maycira Costa studies the Pantanal and learns how life there is affected by changes to the area.	
Text features	Photos: _____ Tables: _____ Diagrams: _____	Photos: _____ Tables: _____ Diagrams: _____

Take turns with a partner. Share what you like about both selections. Share what you like that was in only one of the selections.

Grammar

The Pantanal

Grammar Rules Adjectives

1. Use a **capital letter** for adjectives that describe a country of origin.
2. Add -**er** to the adjective when you compare two things.
3. Add -**est** to the adjective to compare three or more things.
4. Some adjectives have special forms for comparing things. These include **good**, **better**, **best**.

Circle the adjectives. Underline the nouns they describe.

The Brazilian Pantanal is a strange and special place. It is the largest tropical wetland in the world. Many plants and animals live there. Heavy rain falls for months in the Pantanal. This makes the Pantanal green. It is much greener than the dry desert that Elena visited. Scientists want to learn about the amazing Pantanal. They study how human activities affect it. They believe this is the best way to protect the Pantanal for the future.

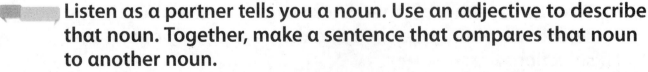 **Listen as a partner tells you a noun. Use an adjective to describe that noun. Together, make a sentence that compares that noun to another noun.**

© Cengage Learning, Inc.

Name _____   Date _____

Characters My Partner Knows

Make a character chart about a story you have read.

Character	Role	Function	Relationship

 Use the chart to describe characters in a story a partner tells you about.

Name _____ Date _____

A Science Report

Grammar Rules Singular and Plural Possessives

1. Possessive nouns tell who owns something.

• For one owner or plural nouns not ending in **-s**, add **'s**

• For more than one owner or nouns ending in **-s**, add only **'**

2. Possessive adjectives do **not** use apostrophes:

my, **your**, **her**, **his**, **its**, **our**, **their**

Circle the correct word.

"(Your, You, Yours) homework for tonight is to write a report about water," Mr. Lee told (her, its, his) students. One (students, student's, students') hand went up in the air.

"Can (my, its, her) report be about the canal behind my house?" asked Josh.

"(Their, My, Your) report can be anything about water," said Mr. Lee.

The next day, the students all had (their, her, your) reports.

"(Me, My, I) report is about water conservation," said Ella. "I wrote about how (peoples, people's, peoples') habits at home can help save water for all of us."

Mr. Lee collected all the (students, students', student's) reports and put them on (his, her, my) desk.

 Use possessive nouns and adjectives to tell a partner about a report you wrote.

© Cengage Learning, Inc.

5.14

Unit 5 | Every Drop

Name _____ Date _____

"My Great-Grandmother's Gourd"

Listen as your teacher reads. Follow with your finger.

1

A village got a new pump. The girl celebrated with the villagers, but her grandmother did not come. She stayed near an old baobab tree.

2

Grandmother was sad. She didn't like the new pump. She said that the villagers used to prepare the trees for the rainy season. Now she only heard the pump. The girl explained that they no longer needed to store water.

3

Grandmother prepared her tree for the rainy season. The villagers laughed. The girl helped her grandmother. Together they worked to fill the tree with water.

4

The dry season came. The pump broke. The girl and her grandmother shared their water.

The next rainy season, all the villagers prepared their trees, just in case the pump broke again.

5.15

The Make-It-Possessive Game

One owner	Add **'s**.	*A village's water is for everyone.*
More than one owner	Add **'** if the noun ends in **-s**.	*The villagers' resources are important.*

1. Play with a partner.

2. Flip a coin. Move one space for heads. Move two spaces for tails.

3. Change the noun to a possessive noun. Say a sentence using the possessive noun.

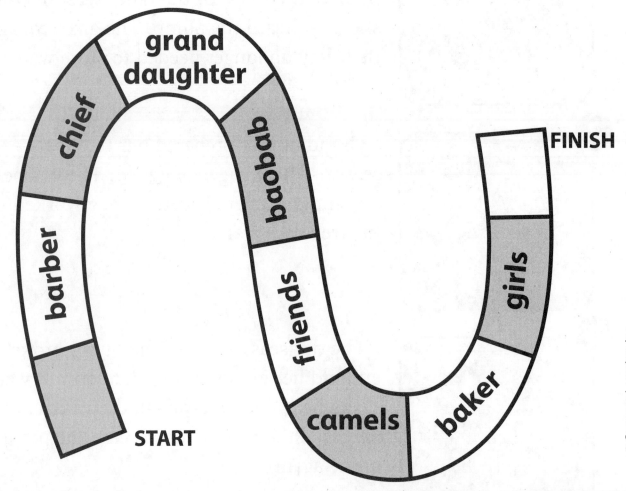

5.16

Make Your Own Game Board

1. Keep the practice going! Make your own game board.

2. In each square, write a noun that names one or more animals, things, or people. Invite a partner to add punctuation to turn the noun into a possessive noun.

With a partner, talk about how you changed the nouns into possessive nouns. Use the rules on page 5.16 if you need help.

Vocabulary

Vocabulary Concentration

1. Write the Key Words from Unit 5 Part 2 and their definitions on separate index cards.

2. Lay all the cards face down. Set the Key Words on the left and the definitions on the right.

3. Flip over one card from each side. If the Key Word and definition match, keep the cards and try to make another match.

4. If the Key Word and definition do not match, put the cards back.

5. Play until all the cards have been matched.

acquire	aquifer	availability	canal
capacity	channel	climate	course
distribution	gourd	region	scarcity
to get	a body of rock that can contain groundwater	the amount of something that is able to be used	a waterway made by people
the maximum amount something can hold	to bring water from one place to another	the general weather conditions in an area	the route or direction followed by water, such as a river
the way something is shared among a group	a container made by hollowing out a fleshy fruit with hard skin	an area, a part of a country	when there is not enough of something, especially a resource

Reread and Retell

"My Great-Grandmother's Gourd"

Use the chart to keep track of each character's role, function, and relationship in "My Great-Grandmother's Gourd."

Character	Role	Function	Relationship
Grandmother	grandmother		
Fatima	granddaughter		

▶ **Use your character chart to retell the story to a partner.**

5.19

Name _____ Date _____

"My Great-Grandmother's Gourd"

Use this passage to practice reading with proper expression.

I looked for my grandmother, who always says she is so proud	12
of me, but I didn't see her. As people pushed forward to try the	26
pump, I pushed outward to find my grandmother.	34
There she stood all alone beneath her best friend, an old	45
baobab tree.	47
"Grandmother, come see the new pump. The water is so easy to	59
get now, our work will be less."	66
Grandmother looked at me, then patted the gnarled trunk of the	77
giant baobab tree with her work-worn hand and said, "Go child.	88
Drink the fresh, cold water. And soon I'll be there, too."	99
I ran back and danced with my friends, celebrating the new	110
pump. But my grandmother did not come.	117

From "My Great-Grandmother's Gourd," page 48

Expression

B ☐ Does not read with feeling.   A ☐ Reads with appropriate feeling for most content.

I ☐ Reads with some feeling, but does not match content.   AH ☐ Reads with appropriate feeling for all content.

Accuracy and Rate Formula

Use the formula to measure a reader's accuracy and rate while reading aloud.

_____ − _____ = _____
words attempted   number of errors   words correct per minute
in one minute   (wcpm)

© Cengage Learning, Inc.

"The Frog That Swallowed All the Water"

Complete the chart.

What I know about the setting and the characters	What I think will happen

▷ **Tell a partner about a prediction you had that was not exactly correct.**

Respond and Extend

Compare Themes

Write *Yes* or *No* to complete the chart.

Themes	"The Frog That Swallowed All the Water"	"My Great-Grandmother's Gourd"
If at first you don't succeed, try and try again.	Yes	
Teamwork works.		Yes
There is more than one way to solve a problem.		
A group is strongest when its members use their different talents.		
Don't give up old ways for new ways.		
Water is important to our lives.		

 Take turns with a partner giving examples from the selection to support your answers.

Name _____ Date _____

The Aquifer's Future

Grammar Rules **Possessive Nouns and Adjectives**

1. When there is only one owner, add **'s** to show ownership.
2. When there is more than one owner and the noun ends in **-s**, just add **'** at the end of the noun.
3. When there is more than one owner and the noun does not end in **-s**, add **'s** at the end of the noun.
4. Possessive adjectives are **my**, **your**, **her**, **his**, **its**, **our**, and **their**.
5. Remember not to use an **apostrophe** with **possessive adjectives**.

Write the correct endings for possessive nouns.

Write possessive adjectives.

All of the town _____ citizens gathered at town hall, anxious to hear _____ mayor speak. _____ speech will be the most important she has ever made. News reporters _____ cameras were ready to film.

"We've had a severe drought this summer and the aquifer in _____ region is drying up. Each community in the region must begin _____ own water-saving policy. It is _____ proposal that we begin water rationing immediately. We must save every drop of water we can now to ensure _____ availability in the future. _____ lives depend on it!"

▭ **Write two new sentences using a possessive noun and a possessive adjective. Discuss your sentences with a partner.**

Name _____   Date _____

Ideas

Writing is well-developed when the message is clear and interesting to the reader. It is supported by details that show the writer knows the topic well.

	Is the message clear and interesting?	Do the details show the writer knows the topic?
4 Wow!	❏ All the writing is clear and focused. ❏ The writing is very interesting.	❏ All the details are about the topic. The writer knows the topic well.
3 Ahh.	❏ Most of the writing is clear and focused. ❏ Most of the writing is interesting.	❏ Most of the details are about the topic. The writer knows the topic fairly well.
2 Hmm.	❏ Some of the writing is not clear. The writing lacks some focus. ❏ Some of the writing is confusing.	❏ Some details are about the topic. The writer doesn't know the topic well.
1 Huh?	❏ The writing is not clear or focused. ❏ The writing is confusing.	❏ Many details are not about the topic. The writer does not know the topic.

Writing Project

Outline

Write the most important ideas on the lines with Roman numerals. Write the details to support each idea on the lines below the Roman numerals.

Outline

I. _____

    A. _____

    B. _____

II. _____

    A. _____

    B. _____

III. _____

    A. _____

    B. _____

Writing Project

Revise

Use revision marks to make changes to this paragraph. Look for places to:

- **add detail**
- **vary sentences**

Revision Marks	
∧	Add
ℒ	Take out
⟲⌢∧	Move to here

Every living thing needs water to survive. Every human needs

water to survive. Water is important? We drink water. We swim in

water. We travel by water. Water has many uses.

Edit and Proofread

Use revision marks to edit and proofread this paragraph. Look for places to use:

- comparatives and superlatives
- adjectives
- apostrophes

Revision Marks	
∧	Add
℘	Take out
⬭ SP	Check spelling
∧ʼ	Add an apostrophe

The Pacific Ocean is huge. It's waters touch many countries. In fact, its the largest ocean on Earth. The second large is the Atlantic Ocean. The Indian Ocean is small than the Atlantic Ocean. All oceans are deep than lakes. The Great Lakes in North America are beautiful. Michigans beaches are on the west coast of Lake Michigan. It's beaches are so beautiful that they are called the United States third coast!

The Wild West

Make a concept map with the answers to the Big Question:
What does it take to settle a new land?

Name _____   Date _____

Identify Causes and Effects

Read "A Long, Cold Night." Then complete the cause-and-effect organizer to show what happened and why.

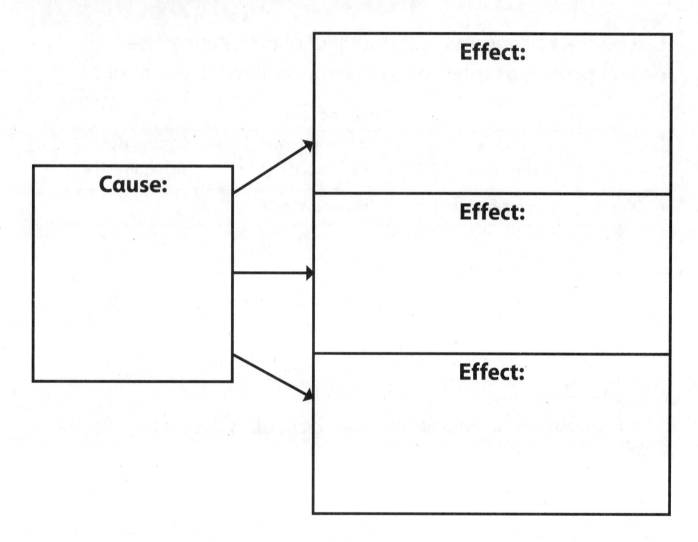

Cause:

Effect:

Effect:

Effect:

Tell a partner which effect you find the most interesting and why.

Grammar

The Lost Calf

Grammar Rules Subject and Object Pronouns

Use **subject pronouns** in the subject of a sentence. Use **object pronouns** after the verb or a small word like *for* or *to*.

Pronouns

	One	More than one	Contractions
Subject	I, she, he, it, you	we, you, they	I'm, you're, it's
Object	me, you, him, her, it	us, you, them	

Say each sentence. Then replace the underlined words with the correct pronoun. Write the pronoun in the blank. Say the new sentence.

1. The cowboy has a male calf. <u>The cowboy</u> guides the calf down a path. _____

2. The cowboy's wife looks for the calf. <u>The cowboy's wife</u> can't find the calf. _____

3. The cowboy and his wife are worried about the calf. <u>The cowboy and his wife</u> search for the calf. _____

4. The cowboy says, "<u>The cowboy</u> will search by the river." _____

5. The cowboy returns without the calf. He could not find <u>the calf</u>. _____

6. The cowboy's wife says, "Here it is! It returned while <u>the cowboy</u> were gone." _____

▭▭▭ **Tell a partner something about yourself. Use the contraction *I'm.***

Name _____ Date _____

"Westward Bound!"

Listen as your teacher reads. Follow with your finger.

1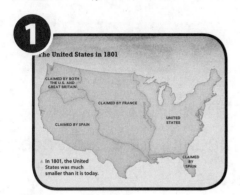

Before 1803, France, Spain, and Britain owned most of the West. Then the Louisiana Purchase was made and President Jefferson sent explorers into the West.

2

Americans first moved to the West because they wanted to own land, get rich, or find adventure.

Gold was discovered in California in 1848. People rushed West, hoping to get rich.

3

Settlers made their homes in California, Oregon, and the Midwest. They soon pushed out the Native Americans.

4

After the Civil War, cattle drives began. Cowboys took cattle from Texas to the north. The open range didn't last long, though. Soon most of the West was settled.

Name _____   Date _____

Grammar

The Reflexive Pronoun Game

Grammar Rules Reflexive Pronouns

1. A **pronoun** is a word that takes the place of a noun.
2. A **reflexive pronoun** refers to the subject of a sentence.
3. A **reflexive pronoun** is necessary for the meaning of a sentence.
4. A **reflexive pronoun** ends in **-self** or **-selves**.
5. These are the **reflexive pronouns**: **myself**, **herself**, **himself**, **itself**, **ourselves**, **themselves**.

1. **Play with a partner.**
2. **Flip a coin. Move one space for heads. Move two spaces for tails.**
3. **Complete the sentence by saying the correct reflexive pronoun. If you are correct, flip the coin again. If you are incorrect, your partner flips the coin.**
4. **The winner is the player who reaches FINISH first.**

She asked _____ when she would feel at home in the West.	He saw _____ on the glassy surface of the water.	The cat purred _____ to sleep.		
I told _____ that the journey west would be exciting.		We enjoyed _____ during the square dance.		FINISH
START		The horses jammed _____ against the fence when they heard the loud noise.	We enjoyed _____ while husking corn.	The settlers placed _____ in the best positions to pan for gold.

© Cengage Learning, Inc.

Vocabulary

Yes or No

Think of a Key Word. Then think of a question you can ask about its meaning. Make sure the question can be answered *yes* or *no*. Read the examples, then write two *yes* or *no* questions of your own.

1. When you explore, do you often discover new things?

2. Does construction mean taking things apart?

3. Do cowboys work in ranching?

4. Did the gold rush happen in the 1900s?

5. Were reservations created for settlers?

6. When there is expansion, are things smaller?

7. When you talk about an individual, are you talking about one person?

8. Did settlers go west to find big cities?

9. _____

10. _____

Reread and Retell

"Westward Bound!"

Read a section of "Westward Bound!" Then complete the cause-and-effect organizer to show an event that happened and the results of the event. Repeat the activity using other sections of "Westward Bound!"

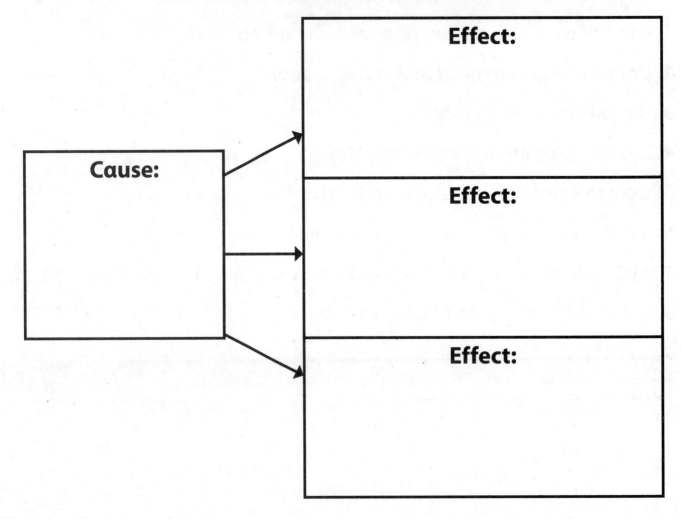

Cause:

Effect:

Effect:

Effect:

◀ Use your organizer to retell the selection to a partner.

Name _____ Date _____

"Westward Bound!"

Use this passage to practice reading with proper intonation.

If you ask anyone about the history of the West, they may tell you about a wild,   17
lawless time, when brave cowboys rode their horses across wide, dusty plains.   29
This is a popular vision of the Old West. It is often shown on TV and in the   47
movies. But it is not the whole story.   55

The real history of the West is much more interesting. It is the story of millions   71
of different kinds of people, all with different ideas about the land and their   85
future on it. They came from many different backgrounds, but they had one   98
thing in common. They lived in a time of great change. It was the time of the   115
westward expansion.   117

From "Westward Bound!," page 90

Intonation

B ☐ Does not change pitch.   A ☐ Changes pitch to match some of the content.

I ☐ Changes pitch, but does not match content.   AH ☐ Changes pitch to match all the content.

Accuracy and Rate Formula

Use the formula to measure a reader's accuracy and rate while reading aloud.

| _____ | − | _____ | = | _____ |
| words attempted in one minute | | number of errors | | words correct per minute (wcpm) |

Name _____   Date _____

"A Day in the Life of a Cowboy"

Complete the strategy planner as you read "A Day in the Life of a Cowboy."

Step 1 What is the author's main purpose for writing?

❑ to tell a story   **OR**   ❑ to give information

❑ to entertain

Step 2 What is your purpose for reading?

❑ for enjoyment   **OR**   ❑ for information

Step 3 What type of story are you going to read?

❑ **fiction**   **OR**   ❑ **nonfiction**

Do the following:	Do the following:
• Identify the characters and settings.	• Read more slowly.
• Think about what happens and when it happens.	• Identify facts about real people or events.
	• Use maps, diagrams, and pictures.
• Use what you know to read new words.	• Concentrate as you read.

▬▬▬ **Tell a partner what you like about the life of a cowboy. Tell what you don't like.**

© Cengage Learning, Inc.

Compare Author's Purpose

Complete the author's purpose chart.

	"A Day in the Life of a Cowboy"	"Westward Bound!"
What was the author's main purpose? • give information or explain • persuade readers • entertain, describe, or express personal feelings • explain how to do something		
How do you know? Give examples.		

Take turns with a partner. Share one question you could ask both authors. Share one question you have for only one author.

Grammar

Lewis and Clark

Grammar Rules Pronoun Agreement

1. Use **I** or **me** to talk about yourself. Use **we** or **us** to talk about yourself and another person.

2. Use **he** or **him** for a boy or man. Use **she** or **her** for a girl or woman. Use **it** for a thing.

3. Use **they** or **them** for two or more people or things. Use **you** to talk to one person or more than one person.

4. Use pairs of pronouns that match in person and number to talk about a person twice in one sentence. (**he**, **himself**)

Circle the nouns. Rewrite the sentence with pronouns in place of the nouns.

1. Sacajawea helped Lewis and Clark. _____

2. Lewis and Clark asked many questions. _____

3. President Jefferson learned a lot because of Sacajawea, too.

_____

4. Lewis and Clark were great teachers. _____

5. Now President Jefferson, the people, and I know a lot about the American West. _____

> Have a partner choose a noun. Tell the noun's number and gender. Then pick a pronoun that can replace the noun. Together, make a sentence using a pair of pronouns with that number and gender.

The Effects of Moving

Make notes in your cause-and-effect chain as a partner tells you about a time when a friend or relative moved away.

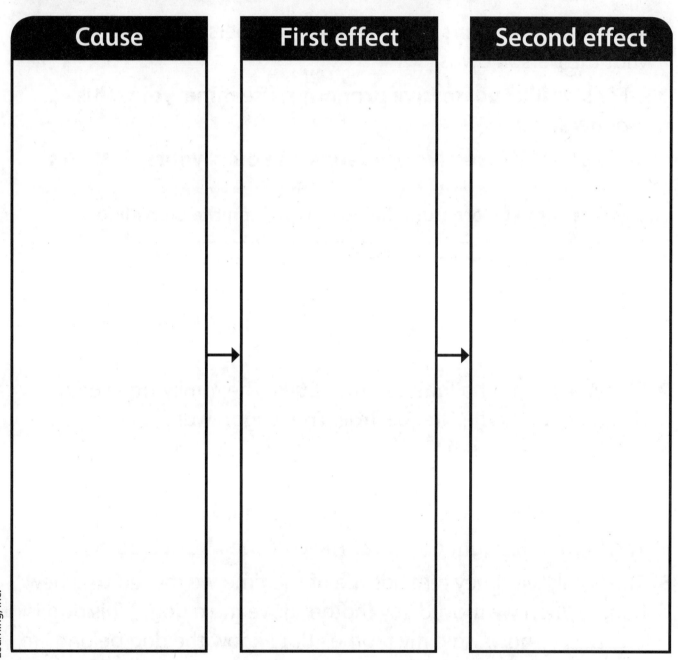

Cause	First effect	Second effect

With a partner, talk about the move. Use your cause-and-effect chain to show what happened because of the move.

Grammar

Our Move Out West

> ## Grammar Rules Singular and Plural Possessive Pronouns
>
> **Possessive pronouns** take the place of a person's name and what the person owns.
>
> 1. For **singular possessive pronouns**, use **mine**, **yours**, **his**, or **hers**.
> 2. For **plural possessive pronouns**, use **ours**, **yours**, or **theirs**.

Choose the correct word from the box. Write it on the blank line.

mine	yours	his	hers	ours	theirs

1. My brother gave me a book for my birthday. The book is _____ .

2. My book is about a family in the 1800s. The family traveled in a wagon along the Oregon Trail. The wagon was _____ .

3. The family had a father, a sister, and a brother. The sister brought a diary. The diary was _____ . She wrote about her pet dog. They had to leave the dog behind when they moved.

4. The brother brought one coat. The coat was _____ .

5. The family's journey reminds me of the time we moved to a new home. When we moved, my mother gave me a dog. "This dog is _____ now," said my mother. But I know the dog belongs to the whole family. The dog is _____ .

Use possessive pronouns to tell a partner about a time you visited a family member or took a trip somewhere.

Key Points Reading

"The Road to Rhyolite"

Listen as your teacher reads. Follow with your finger.

In a desert, two prospectors searched for ore. They discovered gold! They staked their claim and began to mine.

Word traveled fast and soon many people began to arrive. A little town named Rhyolite began to grow. People built homes, stores, banks, hotels, and a school. Soon the population grew.

Then financial problems struck the town. Gold became hard to find. Investors withdrew their money and mines began to close. People left the town and its buildings crumbled. Now Rhyolite is just a ghost town in the desert dust.

Grammar

What or Who Is It?

Grammar Rules Demonstrative and Indefinite Pronouns

1. A **demonstrative pronoun** refers to a specific noun without naming it.
2. An **indefinite pronoun** does not refer to a specific person or thing.

Read each sentence. Underline the demonstrative or indefinite pronoun. Draw a line from each sentence to the type of pronoun used in the sentence.

1. <u>These</u> are not valuable.
2. Does anyone need water?
3. That is shiny.
4. Was anything found in the mine?
5. This is gold.
6. Will somebody get rich?
7. Nobody is in the restaurant.
8. Everyone wants gold.
9. Those are small pieces.
10. That is a new hotel.

Demonstrative Pronoun

Indefinite Pronoun

Grammar

Grammar Rules Demonstrative and Indefinite Pronouns

1. **Demonstrative pronouns**, such as **this, that, these**, and **those** point out specific people, places, or things without naming them.
   Example: **These** are boomtowns.
2. **Indefinite pronouns**, such as **everyone**, **all**, **someone**, and **anything**, do not tell about specific people or things.
   Example: Soon, **everyone** was moving west.

Fill in the blanks with an indefinite or demonstrative pronoun.

During the gold rush, many towns grew quickly. _____

changed many lives. Prospectors dug for gold all over. Where did

they find it? _____ was a secret. However, _____ could

stop others from finding out. It seemed as if _____ in the

world was moving west to look for gold!

At first, towns became boomtowns. Usually, _____ ran out

of gold. After all, _____ can dig for gold, but not _____

can find it or keep it!

Talk with a partner about the pronouns you used. Tell which are indefinite and which are demonstrative.

"The Road to Rhyolite"

Complete the cause-and-effect chains to retell "The Road to Rhyolite" in an order that makes sense.

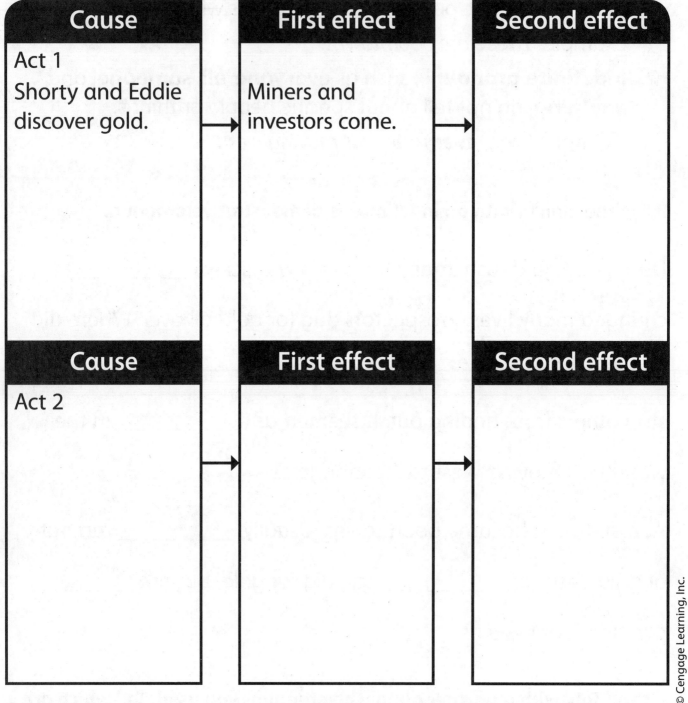

Cause	First effect	Second effect
Act 1 Shorty and Eddie discover gold.	Miners and investors come.	

Cause	First effect	Second effect
Act 2		

Use your cause-and-effect chains to retell the play to a partner.

Name _____ Date _____

"The Road to Rhyolite"

Use this passage to practice reading with proper expression.

AGNES [*to audience*]: Well, here I am again. I know it doesn't seem   13

possible, but two years have passed since I saw you last, and things   26

are changing in Rhyolite.   30

[*Enter miners:* DOYLE, MARY, GISH, *and* YANG. *They look glum.*]   40

MARY [*angrily*]: The mines are drying up and so am I!   51

YANG: There is hardly any gold left in the ground.   61

GISH: There's only dirt and rocks and dirty socks.   70

DOYLE [*sadly*]: Looks like the good times are gone.   79

[*Enter* NEWSBOY *carrying newspapers.*]   83

NEWSBOY: Rhyolite businesses going bankrupt! Read all about it!   92

[AGNES *grabs a newspaper and reads it. Exit* NEWSBOY.]   101

From "The Road to Rhyolite," page 138

Expression

B ☐ Does not read with feeling.   A ☐ Reads with appropriate feeling for most content.

I ☐ Reads with some feeling, but does not match content.   AH ☐ Reads with appropriate feeling for all content.

Accuracy and Rate Formula

Use the formula to measure a reader's accuracy and rate while reading aloud.

$$\underset{\substack{\text{words attempted} \\ \text{in one minute}}}{\underline{\hspace{3cm}}} - \underset{\text{number of errors}}{\underline{\hspace{3cm}}} = \underset{\substack{\text{words correct per minute} \\ \text{(wcpm)}}}{\underline{\hspace{3cm}}}$$

Name _____   Date _____

"Rhyolite: The True Story of a Ghost Town"

Complete the chart as you read "Rhyolite: The True Story of a Ghost Town."

Page	What I read	What it means to me

 Would you have enjoyed living in Rhyolite when it was a boomtown? Tell a partner why or why not.

Name _____   Date _____

Compare Genres

Use a comparison chart to compare a narrative poem and a play.

	Narrative poem	Play
Setting		
Structure and organization Use these words to tell about the organization and structure of the selections: • acts and scenes • dialogue • plot • rhyme • verses		

 In your opinion, which selection told a more powerful story about Rhyolite? Use your chart to help you explain your opinion.

All Aboard!

Grammar Rules Different Kinds of Pronouns

1. **Possessive pronouns mine**, **yours**, **his**, **hers**, **its**, **ours**, and **theirs** show who owns something and what is owned.

   Example: *We found some pickaxes. Are they **yours**?*

2. **Demonstrative pronouns this**, **that**, **these**, and **those** tell about specific people, places, animals, or things without naming them.

   Example: ***These** belong to Shorty and **those** belong to Gish.*

3. **Indefinite pronouns everyone**, **somebody**, **all**, **anybody**, and **anything** do not tell about specific people or things.

   Example: ***Anybody** can dig for gold in Rhyolite.*

Complete each sentence with a possessive, an indefinite, or a demonstrative pronoun.

The train captain shouted, "All aboard _____ ! _____
(indefinite)   (demonstrative)
is the last train out of Rhyolite. We don't want to leave _____
(indefinite)
behind."

Mr. Young anxiously asked his wife, "Do you have your ticket?

_____ is in my pocket. Do the children have _____ ?
(possessive)   (possessive)
We must hurry to catch _____ !"
(demonstrative)

Write three new sentences, each using a different kind of pronoun.
Share your sentences with a partner.

Name _____   Date _____

Voice

Every writer has a special way of saying things, or a voice. The voice should sound genuine, or real, and be unique to that writer.

	Does the writing sound genuine and unique?	**Does the tone fit the audience and purpose?**
4 Wow!	❑ The writing is genuine and unique. It shows who the writer is.	❑ The writer's tone, formal or informal, fits the audience and purpose.
3 Ahh.	❑ Most of the writing sounds genuine and unique.	❑ The writer's tone mostly fits the audience and purpose.
2 Hmm.	❑ Some of the writing sounds genuine and unique.	❑ Some of the writing fits the audience and purpose.
1 Huh?	❑ The writing does not sound genuine or unique.	❑ The writer's tone does not fit the audience or purpose.

Writing Project

Cause-and-Effect Chain

Complete the cause-and-effect chain for your narrative poem.

Cause

⬇

Effect 1

⬇

Effect 2

⬇

Effect 3

⬇

Effect 4

Writing Project

Revise

Use revision marks to make changes to this poem. Look for:

- **a clear and individual voice and style**
- **details about characters and setting**

Revision Marks	
^	Add
℘	Take out

Our wagon moved

On the road.

Our father said,

The wagon could carry a big load.

Name _____   Date _____

Edit and Proofread

Use revision marks to edit and proofread this narrative poem.
Look for:

- **correct pronouns**
- **correct use of quotations and quotation marks**
- **words spelled correctly**

Revision Marks	
∧	Add
℘	Take out
⬯⟋	Move to here
⬯ SP	Check spelling
⟩	Comma
« »	Quotation marks

The Storm

Dad had said "Their is a storm to

come."

Still, she plodded on through mud and ice.

Should we stop the wagon or go ahead?

"Keep on going was Dad's advice.

The wind picked up. It's howl was mighty.

We waited, huddled, for the storm to cease.

By morning it could see the sun.

The storm had stopped. We were at peace.

Unit Concept Map

Talking About Trash

Make a concept map with the answers to the Big Question: Why should we care about garbage?

7.1

Thinking Map

Author's Viewpoint

Complete the author's viewpoint chart about whether students should stay in from recess if their class does not recycle.

Viewpoint	Evidence	Action needed

⬅️ Share your ideas with a partner and listen to his or her ideas. If your ideas are different, see if you can agree on new, better ideas.

© Cengage Learning, Inc.

Grammar

The Class Project

Grammar Rules Adverbs

An **adverb** tells **where**, **when**, or **how**.

Where?	When?	How?
everywhere outside	yesterday daily	easily quickly

Circle the adverbs below. Then categorize them as where, when, or how adverbs.

Today we will start a project. Listen carefully for the directions. First, we will clean the classroom well. Then we will recycle plastic and paper. We will make a container for each. Please put all your bottles there and your paper here. Make sure you wash bottles thoroughly. We will empty the containers weekly.

Where?	When?	How?

Tell a partner one way you can reduce garbage. Use at least two adverbs.

Name _____   Date _____

"The World of Waste"

Listen as your teacher reads. Follow with your finger.

1

Americans throw away a lot of garbage every year. Garbage is building up all over our planet. People need to think about what they buy and what they throw away.

2

Americans produce the most trash. Many other countries produce less trash because they buy less. They reuse more of what they have. Some countries even encourage people to recycle trash.

3

Leftover food and yard waste can be composted. Clothes and electronics can be donated. Jars, bottles, and toys can be reused. Plastic bottles can be recycled into play equipment.

4

You can reduce garbage. Borrow instead of buying. Remember that energy and resources are used to make trash. That's why it should be treated like treasure. Choose items with less packaging. Think of the future.

Grammar

The Comparison Adverb Game

Grammar Rules Adverbs that Compare Actions

1. Use a **comparative adverb** to compare two actions.
2. Form some **comparative adverbs** by adding **-er** to the adverb.
3. Use **more** or **most** with an adverb that ends in **-ly**.
4. Use a **superlative adverb** to compare three or more actions.
5. Form some **superlative adverbs** by adding **-est** to the adverb.

1. **Play with a partner.**
2. **Flip a coin. Move one space for heads, two spaces for tails.**
3. **Complete the sentence by saying the correct form of the adverb. If you are correct, flip the coin again. If you are incorrect, your partner flips the coin.**
4. **The winner is the player who reaches FINISH first.**

He will arrive at the environment club meeting (soon) _____ than his friend will.	Our class recycles paper (carefully) _____ than Mr. Smith's class.	The city's landfill fills up the (rapidly) _____ in the whole state.		
I add to the compost bin (quickly) _____ than you do.		Samir plans projects the (fast) _____ of all.		**FINISH**
START		Tom plans recycling the (skillfully) _____ of all.	Maria works (hard) _____ than Sue does.	You do your pollution research the (happily) _____ of all.

Reread and Retell

"The World of Waste"

Make an author's viewpoint chart for "The World of Waste."

Viewpoint	Evidence	Action needed
Garbage can be good.		

🔊 **Use your chart to retell the author's viewpoint and evidence to a partner. Work with your partner to find additional kinds of evidence the author uses to support her viewpoint. Add them to the evidence column.**

Fluency

"The World of Waste"

Use this passage to practice reading with proper intonation.

Americans win first prize! They produce more garbage than any other country	12
in the world. Look at the graphic on the right. It shows how much trash each	28
person produces in one day, in different countries. Compared with people in	40
the United States, people in other countries produce less trash. How is this	53
possible? They buy fewer things, and reuse and recycle more of them.	65
Some countries even encourage people to recycle. In Switzerland, for example,	76
people have to pay for every bag of garbage they want taken away, but	90
recyclable garbage is taken away for free. Now that's a good reason to recycle!	104

From "The World of Waste," page 174

Intonation

B ☐ Does not change pitch. **A** ☐ Changes pitch to match some of the content.

I ☐ Changes pitch, but does not match content. **AH** ☐ Changes pitch to match all the content.

Accuracy and Rate Formula

Use the formula to measure a reader's accuracy and rate while reading aloud.

$$\underline{\hspace{3cm}} - \underline{\hspace{3cm}} = \underline{\hspace{3cm}}$$

words attempted in one minute	number of errors	words correct per minute (wcpm)

Reading Options

"Message in a Bottle"

Use this page to keep track of the interesting facts you find. Use the fact cards to set up your notes as you find more facts.

That's a fact!

An interesting fact about _____

is _____

I found it in the book _____

by _____

_____   _____
Name   Date

That's a fact!

An interesting fact about _____

is _____

I found it in the book _____

by _____

_____   _____
Name   Date

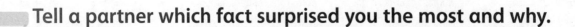 Tell a partner which fact surprised you the most and why.

© Cengage Learning, Inc.

Compare Author's Purpose

Use an author's purpose chart to compare the two selections you have read.

	"The World of Waste"	"Message in a Bottle"
Tell the author's main purpose for each selection.		
List three conclusions about each selection.		
Say how well each author's purpose was achieved.		

Think of a book you like. Tell a partner what the author's purpose for writing was and how you know.

Grammar

Describe It Better

Grammar Rules Adverbs

1. Use an **adverb** to describe a **verb**.
2. Use an **adverb** to tell how often something happens.
3. Use an **adverb** to describe an **adjective** or another **adverb**.

Add an adverb from the list below to tell more about an adverb, adjective, or verb in each sentence. Write the new sentence on the line.

| always | carefully | very | weekly |

1. Some communities are creative about recycling.

_____

2. People collect cans and take them for recycling.

_____

3. They clean the empty cans so they are safe.

_____

4. Some people bring their own bags when they shop.

_____

Tell a partner another creative way to recycle. Use at least one adverb in your sentence.

Name _____ Date _____

A Goal-and-Outcome Plan

Make a goal-and-outcome plan for a story you have read recently.

Somebody (Character(s))	Wanted (Goal)	But (Obstacle(s))	So (Outcome)

 Work with a partner. Tell them about the goals, obstacles, and outcomes in a story you have read recently.

Trash Day

Grammar Rules Prepositions

A **preposition** is a connecting word in a phrase that can tell where, show direction, or show time.

- prepositions that tell where: **in, on, over, by, near**
- prepositions that show direction: **to, into, around, across, down, through**
- prepositions that show time: **before, during, after**

Choose prepositions from the box below to correctly fill in each blank.

after	by	during	before	in	down	over	near

My family makes an effort to dispose of their garbage _____

the day. We do not like to put the trash cans out _____ dark.

Twice a week _____ breakfast, the garbage truck comes

_____ my house. The workers pick up our trash and drive

_____ the block. They dispose of the trash _____ the landfill.

The landfill is _____ the bridge _____ the end of town.

Tell a partner where and when you might pick up litter. Have your partner name the prepositions you used.

© Cengage Learning, Inc.

"Where I Live"

Listen as your teacher reads. Follow with your finger.

1

Elena is writing a report about garbage. From her window, she can see kids littering. She wonders if the kids know about recycling.

2

Elena goes to the store with her reusable shopping bag. Her friend Ricky goes with her. The grocer gives them gum. Ricky throws his wrapper on the ground. Angrily, Elena picks it up. Later, outside her apartment building, she starts counting the pieces of gum stuck to the steps.

3

Elena goes home to finish her report. She thinks of all the gum and trash on her street. She knows most of it could be recycled. She imagines using compost in a flower box to brighten the environment.

Name ____________________ Date ____________

Grammar

Preposition Story

Grammar Rules **Prepositional Phrases**

1. A **prepositional phrase** starts with a preposition and ends with a noun or pronoun.
2. The noun or pronoun is the object of the preposition.

1. **Copy these words onto index cards. Lay them out face down.**
2. **Divide the cards evenly between you and a partner.**
3. **Tell a story about a piece of garbage on a journey.**
4. **The player who uses all of his or her cards wins!**

in front of	over	under	between
on	beside	across	over
next to	into	through	around
off	against	toward	in

Tell a partner where you put garbage. Have your partner name the prepositional phrases in your sentences.

"Where I Live"

Make a goal-and-outcome plan to show whether Elena's plan for her neighborhood succeeds.

Somebody (Character(s))	Wanted (Goal)	But (Obstacle(s))	So (Outcome)
Elena			

Work with a partner. Tell what clues you used to figure out Elena's goals and obstacles. Then work together to talk about Ricky's goals and obstacles. Add them to your chart.

Fluency

"Where I Live"

Use this passage to practice reading with proper intonation.

"Hey," I call to Ricky, who is now by himself. Where did Pablo	13
What's-His-Name go? Maybe his mother called him—mothers are	24
always yelling from open windows, "Come inside! It's time to eat!"	35
Ricky, whose shoelaces are undone, joins me, the marbles	44
clicking in his pocket with each step.	51
You're probably thinking, do I LIKE Ricky? No. He's smaller	61
than me, only seven years old, and likes marbles and his army men.	74
Also, if he were to show you his knees, you would see that they have	89
scabs the color of bacon. I don't have scabs, and unlike Ricky, who	102
always has snot sliding out of his nostrils, I almost never catch colds. And if I	118
do, I use tissue and dispose of it properly.	127

From "Where I Live," page 211

Intonation

B	☐ Does not change voice	A	☐ Changes voice to match some of the content
I	☐ Changes voice, but it does not match content	AH	☐ Changes voice to match all the content

Accuracy and Rate Formula

Use the formula to measure a reader's accuracy and rate while reading aloud.

_____	−	_____	=	_____
words attempted in one minute		number of errors		words correct per minute (wcpm)

Respond and Extend

Alike and Different!

Compare and contrast Sarah Cynthia Sylvia Stout and Elena Gomez from the two selections. Then complete the Venn diagram.

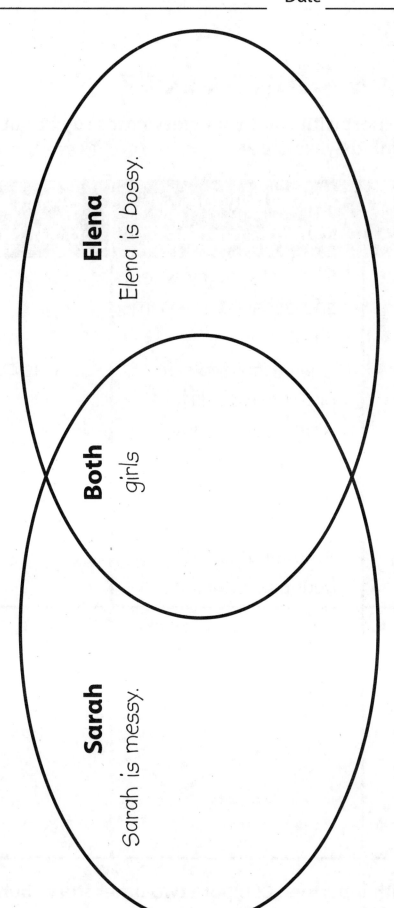

Sarah

Sarah is messy.

Both

girls

Elena

Elena is bossy.

Talk with a partner. Compare two other story characters you know about.

Name _____   Date _____

Compare Characters

Complete the chart with what your classmates say about Elena Gomez and Sarah Cynthia Sylvia Stout.

Character	What the character does	What this shows about the character
Elena	• She gets angry when she sees waste on the street. • She tells people to pick up their litter. • She dreams about choosing an ice cream flavor. • She dreams about a flower box with beautiful flowers.	• She is bossy.
Sarah		

Talk with a partner. Compare two other story characters you know about.

Grammar

Ricky's Story

Grammar Rules Prepositional Phrases

1. Use **prepositional phrases** to show <u>location</u>:
   *Ricky played **near** Elena's apartment.*

2. Use **prepositional phrases** to show <u>direction</u>:
   *Elena and Ricky headed **down** the street.*

3. Use **prepositional phrases** to show <u>time</u>:
   ***After** school, Ricky plays marbles with his cousin Pablo.*

4. Use **prepositional phrases** to give <u>details</u>:
   *Elena wrote a report **about** recycling.*

Write prepositional phrases.

My name is Ricky, and I live _____ as Elena.

I play marbles _____ after school every day.

One day _____, Elena asked me to go with

her _____ to buy eggs and milk. When we

saw the ice cream treats _____, we dreamed

_____. When Elena paid for the eggs and milk,

Mr. Asmara gave us some gum. Elena yelled at me when I threw

the gum wrapper _____. She taught me an

important lesson: Don't litter!

▨ **Tell a partner about places where you can find litter. Use prepositional phrases in your sentences.**

Writing Project

Ideas

Writing is well-developed when the message is clear and interesting to the reader. It is supported by details that show the writer knows the topic well.

	Is the message clear and interesting?	Do the details show the writer knows the topic?
4 Wow!	❑ All the writing is clear and focused. ❑ The writing is very interesting.	❑ All the details are about the topic. The writer knows the topic well.
3 Ahh.	❑ Most of the writing is clear and focused. ❑ Most of the writing is interesting.	❑ Most of the details are about the topic. The writer knows the topic fairly well.
2 Hmm.	❑ Some of the writing is not clear. The writing lacks some focus. ❑ Some of the writing is confusing.	❑ Some details are about the topic. The writer doesn't know the topic well.
1 Huh?	❑ The writing is not clear or focused. ❑ The writing is confusing.	❑ Many details are not about the topic. The writer does not know the topic.

Author's Viewpoint Chart

Complete the author's viewpoint chart for your persuasive essay.

Viewpoint	Evidence	Action needed

Revise

Use revision marks to make changes to these paragraphs. Look for:

- a clearly stated opinion
- reasons, facts, and examples that support the opinion
- a clear statement about the action people should take

Revision Marks	
∧	Add
℘	Take out

Water to Survive

Every living thing needs water to survive. Every human needs water to survive.

Water is important. When the quality of water changes, it changes the health of living things. We should do many things to help with water on Earth. Everyone can do something.

Writing Project

Edit and Proofread

Use revision marks to edit and proofread this paragraph. Look for:

- **correct spelling of adverbs**
- **correct use of adverbs**
- **correct use of semi-colons and colons**

Revision Marks	
∧	Add
℘	Take out
⬭ SP	Check spelling
≡	Capitalize
∧ˏ	Add an apostrophe

Let's reuse old wood and other materials for our gardens! Every

Saturday, I go with my uncle to look for things people no longer

want. We oftener pick up pieces of wood and old windows we

can easyly use these to build a greenhouse. We sometimesly

find these items, too cardboard, paper, bins, and boxes. We use

these materials for soil. We clean out garages and find all kinds of

cool things. I real love using old things to make new things!

One Idea

**Make a concept map with the answers to the Big Question:
How can one idea change your future?**

Name _____ Date _____

Steps in a Process

Use a sequence chain to explain the steps you would take to start a business.

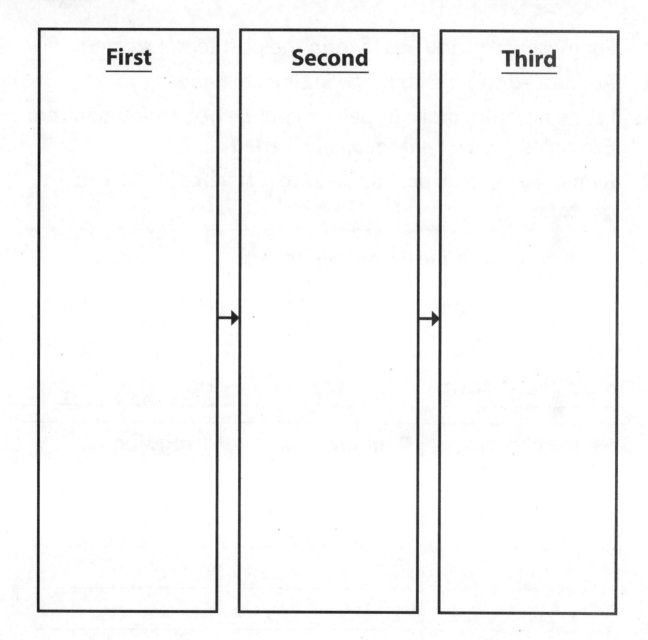

First	Second	Third

Use a sequence chain to tell a partner the steps that you would take to start a business. Use the words *first, second,* and *third* to explain the steps in an order that makes sense.

Name _____ Date _____

It Happened Yesterday

Grammar Rules Regular and Irregular Past Tense Verbs

1. For most verbs, add **-ed** to form the past tense: **start_ed_.**

2. Add just **-d** to verbs that end in silent **e**: **bake_d_**

3. For some verbs, make a spelling change before you add **-ed**: Examples: plan → **plan_ned_**; try → **tr_ied_**

4. Remember special past tense forms for verbs like **is**, **are**, **do**, **go**, **take**.

Categorize the verbs. Write the past tense verb.

do	look	cook	save	give
fry	like	take	touch	taste
play	form	dry	go	is

Spelling change	Regular	Irregular
	cooked	

Use three of the verbs above. Tell a partner something you did last week.

Grammar

We Took Steps to Success!

Grammar Rules Past Tense Verbs

1. Add just **-d** to verbs that end in silent **e**: bake → **baked**
2. Double the final consonant for verbs that end in vowel + consonant: plan → **planned**
3. Change **y** to **i** and add **-ed** for verbs that end in consonant + *y*: try → **tried**

Rewrite each sentence changing the verb to the past tense.

1. We <u>have</u> ideas for new businesses. _____
2. We <u>list</u> all the ideas on paper. _____
3. Soon, we <u>decide</u> which idea <u>is</u> best. _____
   _____
4. Everyone <u>is</u> excited! _____
5. We <u>hurry</u> to the computer. _____
6. Step by step, we <u>follow</u> a process. _____
   _____
7. As a result, we <u>succeed</u> in business! _____
   _____
8. We <u>are</u> proud. _____

 Talk with a partner about the steps you followed to change present tense verbs to past tense verbs.

"Starting Your Own Business: Seven Steps to Success"

Listen as your teacher reads. Follow with your finger.

1

Many kids start businesses to earn money. They start and manage many types of businesses. It's usually both challenging and fun.

2

To start your own business, first make a plan. Decide what type of business to run. List the materials you need and determine your start-up costs. Raise your start-up money. Set the right price for your goods and services and then advertise your new business.

3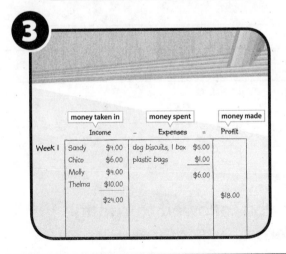

It is important to keep track of your income and expenses. You should also figure your profit. Have an adult check your work to be sure everything is correct.

Grammar

The Present Perfect Tense Game

Grammar Rules Present Perfect Tense

1. A present perfect verb tells about an action that happened at an indefinite time in the past and may still be happening.

2. Form a present perfect verb with a present tense form of **have** and the **past participle**.

3. A **past participle** usually ends in **-ed**, but there are some irregular past participles.

1. **Play with a partner.**

2. **Spin the spinner.**

3. **Read the sentence. Fill in the blank with the correct present perfect verb.**

Make a Spinner

1. Place one loop of a paper clip over the center of the circle.

2. Push a sharp pencil through the loop and the paper.

3. Spin the paper clip around the pencil.

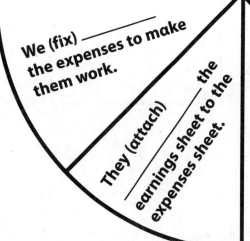
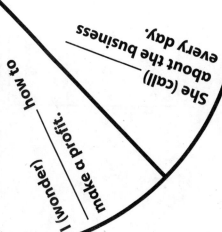

Pat (want) _____ to start a business for a long time.

He (count) _____ the profits every week.

Maria and Dave (start) _____ a new yard business.

Lee (warn) _____ against starting a business too quickly.

She (call) _____ about the business every day.

We (fix) _____ the expenses to make them work.

They (attach) _____ the earnings sheet to the expenses sheet.

I (wonder) _____ how to make a profit.

Name _____   Date _____

"Starting Your Own Business"

Make a sequence chain about "Starting Your Own Business."

How to Plan Your Business

First	**Second**	**Third**
Think about your business goals. →	→	

▸ **Use your organizer to explain the procedure to a partner.**

8.7

Name _____   Date _____

"Starting Your Own Business"

Use this passage to practice reading with proper phrasing.

Have you ever dreamed of having lots of money of your own?   12
Then you should think about starting a business. Every year, thousands   23
of kids start businesses. They earn extra money to spend or to save.   36
Some kids use their business earnings to pay for trips, lessons, or   48
for college later on. Kids do more than just babysit or mow lawns.   61
Many kids have found ways to make their businesses different   71
and special.   73

People who start and manage their own businesses are   82
entrepreneurs. Entrepreneurs are good planners and organizers.   89
Before starting a business, an entrepreneur finds a need and thinks   100
about how to fill it. Starting a business isn't always easy, but it's usually   114
challenging and fun.   117

From "Starting Your Own Business," pages 246–247

Phrasing

| B ☐ Rarely pauses while reading the text. | A ☐ Frequently pauses at appropriate points in the text. |
| I ☐ Occasionally pauses while reading the text. | AH ☐ Consistently pauses at all appropriate points in the text. |

Accuracy and Rate Formula

Use the formula to measure a reader's accuracy and rate while reading aloud.

_____ – _____ = _____
words attempted   number of errors   words correct per minute
in one minute   (wcpm)

Name _____ Date _____

Questions About a Business

Fill in the chart with questions and answers about a business.

Page	My question	The answer

Ask a partner one of your questions. Then try to answer your partner's question.

Compare Procedures

List the steps for starting a business from "Starting Your Own Business."
Then check the steps that were followed by Kayla Legare.

Steps in "Starting Your Own Business"	Steps Kayla Legare used
1. Plan your business	✓
2.	
3.	
4.	
5.	
6.	
7.	

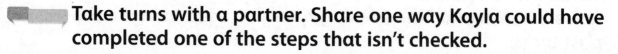 **Take turns with a partner. Share one way Kayla could have completed one of the steps that isn't checked.**

Grammar

Kayla's Menus

Grammar Rules Regular and Irregular Past Tense Verbs

1. For most verbs, add **-ed** to form the past tense: **started**.
2. Add just **-d** to verbs that end in silent **e**: **baked**.
3. Double the final consonant for verbs that end in vowel + consonant: **fanned**.
4. Change **y** to **i** and add **-ed** for verbs that end with consonant + y: **tried**.
5. Remember special past tense forms for **is**, **are**, **do**, **go**, **take**.

Complete the passage by writing the verbs in the past tense.

Kayla _____ special software to make menus for blind and
(use)

visually impaired people. She _____ her business with her uncle.
(plan)

He _____ interested and wanted to help her. They _____ to
(is)   (go)

talk to restaurant owners. Kayla _____ that no one would buy
(worry)

her menus. She and her uncle _____ happy that restaurants
(are)

bought the menus.

Listen when a partner tells you a verb. Say the verb in the past tense. Then explain the spelling rules you used to make the past tense.

Story Map

Use a story map to show the different parts of a story you know.

Characters	**Setting**

Plot

Theme

Retell the story to a partner using your story map.

Grammar

At the Bank

Grammar Rules Past Progressive

The **past progressive** tells about an action that was happening over a period of time in the past. To form the **past progressive**:
- use helping verbs **was**, **were**
- add **-ing** to the main verb

Write the past progressive form of the verb shown below each line.

1. An entrepreneur _____ for a loan from the bank.
      (ask)

2. The bank teller _____ out the paper work.
      (fill)

3. Another entrepreneur _____ money for a new business.
      (borrow)

4. Many other customers _____ in line.
      (standing)

5. They _____ to get credit from the bank, too.
      (wait)

6. They _____ about their new ideas.
      (think)

7. Across the country, new businesses _____ every day.
      (start)

8. Customers _____ new goods and services.
      (buy)

Use the past progressive to tell a partner about what you did when you had a good idea.

Name _____ Date _____

"The Music Maker"

Listen as your teacher reads. Follow with your finger.

1

Ying Yue and her family are poor. They sell fish at the market, but they don't have enough money to eat fish at home. Ying Yue loves making musical instruments from objects she finds at the market.

2

One day, Ying Yue sold a drum she had made. A couple of days later, she sold a tambourine. She made more instruments and sold all of them, too.

3

Ying Yue decided to teach other stallholders how to make the instruments. In exchange for classes, they each gave Ying Yue three fish. When they couldn't find the pieces they needed for the instruments, Ying Yue asked Mrs. Zhang for a loan to buy parts.

4

Ying Yue stocked her grandmother's fish tanks, but no customers were coming to the market. Then Ying Yue heard music. The stallholders were playing their instruments. Customers started coming to the market, and Ying Yue's grandmother sold all her fish.

Grammar

The Make-It-Perfect Game

Grammar Rules Past Perfect and Present Perfect

1. The **present perfect tense** describes an action that began in the past that may continue. It uses the helping verbs **have** and **has**.

2. The **past perfect tense** tells about an action that was completed before some other action in the past. It uses the helping verb **had**.

applied	gone	hired	started	sold	built
helped					agreed
bought					traveled
worked					carried
used					grown
wanted					borrowed
START		FINISH	succeeded	loaned	changed

1. Play with a partner.
2. Flip a coin. Move one space for heads. Move two spaces for tails.
3. Say a sentence about "The Music Maker" using the past perfect or present perfect form of the verb. If you use the verb correctly, flip the coin again.
4. To win, reach the FINISH first!

© Cengage Learning, Inc.

"The Music Maker"

Fill in the story map for "The Music Maker."

```
┌─────────────────────────┐     ┌─────────────────────────┐
│     Characters          │     │        Setting          │
│  Ying Yue               │     │                         │
│                         │     │                         │
│                         │     │                         │
└─────────────────────────┘     └─────────────────────────┘
```

```
┌───────────────────────────────────────────────────────────┐
│                      Beginning                            │
│  Ying Yue discovers that people are interested in her      │
│  musical instruments.                                      │
└───────────────────────────────────────────────────────────┘
```

```
┌───────────────────────────────────────────────────────────┐
│                        Middle                             │
│                                                           │
│                                                           │
└───────────────────────────────────────────────────────────┘
```

```
┌───────────────────────────────────────────────────────────┐
│                         End                               │
│                                                           │
│                                                           │
```

Theme

Use your story map to retell the story to a partner. Tell how you decided what the theme was.

Name _____   Date _____

"The Music Maker"

Use this passage to practice reading with proper expression.

Ying Yue began giving classes in the nearby public park every	11
afternoon after the marketplace had closed. Many stallholders came	20
to her classes. They brought all sorts of things to class, from empty	33
oil cans to cardboard boxes and string from recycled fabric. Ying Yue	45
taught them how to make instruments from all the different materials.	56
However, Ying Yue realized that they couldn't always find all the	67
pieces they needed for the instruments.	73
"I have an idea," Ying Yue announced to Nai Nai. "I am going to	87
buy the parts we can't find from Mrs. Zhang."	96
"But how will you pay Mrs. Zhang for the parts?" asked Nai Nai.	109
Ying Yue thought for a couple of minutes and then answered,	120
"I will ask her for a loan. We can pay her back when we sell all the	137
fish that we'll be getting from the stallholders."	145

From "The Music Maker," page 285

Expression

B	☐ Does not read with feeling.	A	☐ Reads with appropriate feeling for most content.
I	☐ Reads with some feeling, but does not match content.	AH	☐ Reads with appropriate feeling for all content.

Accuracy and Rate Formula

Use the formula to measure a reader's accuracy and rate while reading aloud.

_____ − _____ = _____
words attempted   number of errors   words correct per minute
in one minute   (wcpm)

Strategy Planner

Complete the strategy planner as you read "Another Way of Doing Business."

Step ❶ What is the author's main purpose for writing this

magazine article?

❏ to tell a story   **OR**   ❏ to give information

❏ to entertain

Step ❷ What is your main purpose for reading?

❏ for enjoyment   **OR**   ❏ for information

Step ❸ What type of selection are you going to read?

❏ **fiction**   **OR**   ❏ **nonfiction**

Do the following:
- Identify the characters and settings.
- Think about what happens and when it happens.

Do the following:
- Identify the topic.
- Study maps and pictures.
- Read labels.

Predict what this selection will be about. After reading, confirm or revise your prediction with a partner.

Respond and Extend

Compare Ideas

Use a comparison chart to compare the two texts.

	"Another Way of Doing Business"	"The Music Maker"
Name the businesses.		Musical instruments
Who started it?		Ying Yue
Where did the start-up costs come from?	A small-business loan	
Name the start-up materials.		
Do you think it will continue to be successful? Why?		

◄ **Talk with a partner about ways businesses can help people.**

Grammar

Ana's Dream

Grammar Rules Future Tense Verbs

1. Use **will + main verb** to tell about the future.
   I **will go** to market in the morning. She **will go** with me.
2. Use **be + going to + main verb** to tell about the future.
   I **am going to buy** firewood. She **is going to buy** tools.

Write future tense verbs. Use both rules.

Ana was tired of her job. Her dream was to be her own boss.

Ana thought to herself, "Tomorrow, I _____ to the
                                                                (Rule 1: go)
bank and ask for a loan. I _____ my own business.
                                               (Rule 2: start)
I _____ a learning center for young children."
      (Rule 1: open)

At first, the banker did not want to give Ana a loan, but Ana said,

"I _____ hard, and you _____ that I
      (Rule 1: work)   (Rule 1: find)
_____ my loan quickly." The banker knew that Ana
   (Rule 2: repay)
would keep her word. "You _____ your loan," he said.
                                          (Rule 1: get)
"Together, we _____ sure your business succeeds."
                      (Rule 2: make)

   Tell a partner what you would like to do for work when you are
   older. Use both rules in your sentences.

© Cengage Learning, Inc.

Writing Project

Voice

Every writer has a special way of saying things, or a voice. The voice should sound genuine, or real, and be unique to that writer.

	Does the writing sound genuine and unique?	**Does the tone fit the audience and purpose?**
4 Wow!	❑ The writing is genuine and unique. It shows who the writer is.	❑ The writer's tone, formal or informal, fits the audience and purpose.
3 Ahh.	❑ Most of the writing sounds genuine and unique.	❑ The writer's tone mostly fits the audience and purpose.
2 Hmm.	❑ Some of the writing sounds genuine and unique.	❑ Some of the writing fits the audience and purpose.
1 Huh?	❑ The writing does not sound genuine or unique.	❑ The writer's tone does not fit the audience or purpose.

Name _____   Date _____

Sequence Chain

Complete the sequence chain for a procedure.

Procedure name: _____

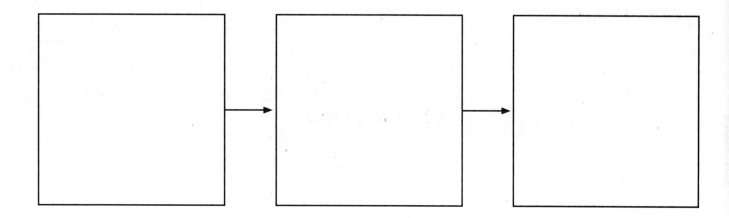

Writing Project

Revise

Use revision marks to make changes to these paragraphs. Look for:

- a clear statement of the procedure
- logical order of steps
- strong voice

Revision Marks	
∧	Add
℘	Take out
⌒➞	Move to here

Clothing Drive

You can get rid of old clothes. Here's what to do.

First, locate and call the used clothing drop-off center in your city. Finally, take the old clothes you find to the drop-off center. Then look in your home for old clothes.

By following this procedure, we can help other people in our city.

Try it.

Edit and Proofread

Use revision marks to edit and proofread these paragraphs.
Look for:

- **correct use of future tense**
- **correct use of commas with introductory words and phrases**
- **correct use of irregular verb forms**

Revision Marks	
∧	Add
⌄	Add comma
ℐ	Take out

Let's ask our local city government about the coins in the fountains! We can sponsor an event to collect money for a charity. First we can choose a charity to donate the money to. After that we can write a plan. Next, we can send our plan to a radio station.

We hope people going to throw more coins in the fountain for a good cause. Last week we do all our work getting ready for the project.

On the day of the event we can take pictures of people throwing coins into the fountain. We very excited to gather the coins and show people helping our community.

Photographic Credits

5.4 (t) Stockbyte/Getty Images. (b) Thomas J. Abercrombie/National Geographic/Getty Images. 6.4 (tc) Hulton Archive/Archive Photos/Getty Images. (b) GRANGER / GRANGER. 7.1 (t) High Impact Photography/ Shutterstock. 7.4 (bc) Emma Peios/Alamy Stock Photo. (bl) Martin Lee / Alamy Stock Photo. (bc) Martin Lee / Alamy Stock Photo. (br) Warren Diggles/Alamy Stock Photo.